Money for Your Life

Invest in Your Financial Future

Home Ownership

Higher Education

DES

LEARN

Stock Market

$

$

$

INVESTING YOUR MONEY

By Diane Dakers

Educational Consultant:
Christopher A. Fons, M.A.
Social Studies and Economics Faculty
Milwaukee Public Schools

Crabtree Publishing Company
www.crabtreebooks.com

Financial Literacy for Life

Author: Diane Dakers

Series research and development: Reagan Miller

Project coordinator: Mark Sachner, Water Buffalo Books

Editorial director: Kathy Middleton

Editors: Mark Sachner, Janine Deschenes

Proofreader: Wendy Scavuzzo

Photo research: Westgraphix/Tammy West

Designer: Westgraphix/Tammy West

Production coordinator and prepress technician:
  Tammy McGarr

Print coordinator: Margaret Amy Salter

Contributing writer and editor: Christopher A. Fons,
economics teacher, Riverside University High School,
Milwaukee Public Schools

Written and produced for Crabtree Publishing Company by
Water Buffalo Books

Photographs:

Front cover: All images from Shutterstock

Interior:

Shutterstock: pp. 1, 3, 4, 5, 6, 8, 9, 10, 11, 12, 13, 14, 16, 18, 21,
  23, 24, 25, 26, 27, 28, 29, 32, 33, 34, 35, 36, 37, 38, 39, 40, 41,
  42, 43; Alexey Boldin: p. 19 (right).

Water Buffalo Books/Westgraphix: p. 19 (left).

Library and Archives Canada Cataloguing in Publication

Dakers, Diane, author
    Money for your life : invest in your financial future / Diane Dakers.

(Financial literacy for life)
Includes index.
Issued in print and electronic formats.
ISBN 978-0-7787-3098-9 (hardcover).--
ISBN 978-0-7787-3107-8 (softcover).--
ISBN 978-1-4271-1877-6 (HTML)

    1. Finance, Personal--Juvenile literature. 2. Investments--Juvenile
literature. I. Title.

HG179.D3436 2017   j332.024   C2016-907143-X
                                            C2016-907144-8

Library of Congress Cataloging-in-Publication Data

CIP available at the Library of Congress

Crabtree Publishing Company

www.crabtreebooks.com   1-800-387-7650

Printed in Canada/062017/MA20170420

Published in Canada
Crabtree Publishing
616 Welland Ave.
St. Catharines, Ontario
L2M 5V6

Published in the United States
Crabtree Publishing
PMB 59051
350 Fifth Avenue, 59th Floor
New York, New York 10118

Published in the United Kingdom
Crabtree Publishing
Maritime House
Basin Road North, Hove
BN41 1WR

Published in Australia
Crabtree Publishing
3 Charles Street
Coburg North
VIC 3058

Contents

CHAPTER ONE

MUCH ADO ABOUT SPENDING & SAVING

Psst...want to know the number-one rule of managing money? Don't spend more than you have. Of course, that's easier said than done. What if you really need something but don't have the money needed to pay for it? Then you have to make some decisions. Is it really something you need, or do you just want it? How can you buy it if you don't have the cash?

So many things to pay for, but only so much money to pay them with. How do you decide what is a need and what is a want? Should you borrow to pay for something? Learning how money works can help you budget what you have, plan for the future, and make wise choices.

Being Smart With Money

Making money decisions doesn't have to be difficult. It's important to have a basic knowledge of math and a handle on how money is made before you can spend it wisely. Saving wisely is also important. You want to make the most of your money. Luckily, there are many ways to do so.

Money: A challenging relationship

Many people have an awkward relationship with money. We live in a world where we are all **consumers**. We all need basic items such as food, shelter, and clothing. Most of us pay for these basic needs. If we have enough money left over, we might spend it on something we want. Some people have more than enough money to pay for basic needs, as well as satisfy all their wants. Other people don't have enough money to meet basic needs.

EDUCATION

SHOPPING

AUTO LOANS

HEALTH & MEDICINE

HOME LOANS

TRAVEL

FOOD

CREDIT CARD BILLS

WATER BILL

ELECTRICITY BILL

TRANSPORATION

FUEL

INTERNET

PHONE BILL

COFFEE

MONEY SAVING

CREDIT CARD

Shown here are some of the expenses that you may have to pay every month when you become an adult. As you become more financially independent, you will need to sit down and balance costs such as these. It's all a part of becoming financially savvy!

Where Your Money Comes From

Take a look in your purse, wallet, or back pocket. Are you flush with cash? Likely not, unless you are fortunate enough to have wealthy parents or a generous grandparent. Most people work hard to earn their money. Knowing where your money comes from is one of the first steps to managing it. An allowance, a part-time job, and gifts are all sources of money.

Most allowances are given by parents or caregivers. They are set amounts that may be tied to some form of work, such as chores. Jobs are usually paid hourly, so that you get a set amount per hour worked. That money is ongoing for as long as the job lasts. If you are lucky, you may get gifts of money for your birthday, or Christmas. These gifts are great but they are temporary. Once you have a handle on where your money comes from, you can put a value on it. It will help you make smart decisions about what to do with your money.

Whether they are talking about buying a gift for a friend or getting a **loan** to buy a new car, for most adults, money is a part of the conversation of everyday life. And learning the language of money is a big step on the path to financial literacy and success.

$PEAKING OF MONEY ...
"Teaching kids sound financial habits at an early age gives all kids the opportunity to be successful when they are an adult."

Warren Buffett, influential business executive
known for his financial skill and generous
support of charitable causes

Learn the Language of Money

Financial literacy is about learning the language of money and becoming comfortable speaking that language. It's about understanding how to earn money, keep track of it, and save and spend it wisely. Mostly, financial literacy is about learning how money works–and how it can work for you.

Many people consider money a **taboo** subject or something that is not acceptable to talk about in public. Not talking about money, though, can lead to financial problems in life.

Living Close to The Edge

More than half of all American adults live "**paycheck-to-paycheck**." That means they receive a paycheck at work, spend their money on bills and necessities, and have nothing left until the next payday. They never get ahead. They can never save for something special. They never set aside a stash of cash for emergencies. It's a frustrating way to live.

There are many factors that contribute to living paycheck-to-paycheck. Some have to do with declining wages and job opportunities, and higher costs of food and housing. Others involve inequality between wealthy members of society and the "working poor" who live in poverty even though they have jobs. There are also historic and stubborn cycles of poverty that so many people cannot break free from, no matter how hard they work.

Many of these factors lie beyond the control of average citizens. For example, money is often passed down within families, meaning that the same people will stay wealthy. These people often have the cash to start businesses and make a lot more money.

Sometimes, job opportunities are only available to people who live in certain expensive cities. Still, there are ways that can help prevent people from living paycheck-to-paycheck. One great way to fight falling into this cycle is to launch your financial literacy learning ASAP.

Thinking Ahead

That might sound crazy. Why start thinking about any of this stuff now? After all, you're just a kid—and you have hardly any money to manage anyway.

What you do have, though, is lots of time and little to lose! That makes this the *perfect* time to start mastering money matters.

It isn't as complicated as you might think. Getting an A+ in Financial Literacy 101 means thinking about the things you want and need in life, and coming up with plans to get those things. It's about balancing spending money with saving money. It means knowing where your money comes from and where it goes.

If Only...

Most adults say they wish they'd started learning about money and saving earlier in life. Now's your chance to learn for yourself, so you can avoid living paycheck-to-paycheck.

With financial literacy, you can set yourself up for a lifetime of commanding your coinage, mastering your moolah, dominating your dough...you get the idea. If you set up your sense about dollars now, it's less likely you'll be singing the money blues later.

Now is a good time to start learning the basics of financial literacy. Something as simple as saving small amounts of money can be the first step on the path to a financial education.

CAN'T BUY ME LOVE

People show their love for one another in different ways–from shouting it from the rooftops to caring for friends and family by helping them with daily tasks.

Some people buy expensive gifts to show they cherish another person. Gifts can be a sweet gesture, a **tangible** expression of love and affection. But costly gifts can sometimes blind their recipient.

Be wary of people who *only* show they care by giving expensive gifts. Some people spend money to "prove" they love someone–but offer no other loving gestures. They might buy presents to make up for bad behavior. Or maybe they spend money instead of spending time with others.

Buying a special gift for someone special is a generous act. But giving gifts should never become the chief measure of people's affection for one another. Friendship and love are the real treasures. They are not things to be bought and sold.

MONEY MATTERS

From the first time you get an allowance, until long after you **retire** from your future career, money will be a constant in your life. You'll save some and you'll spend some. You'll put some in a **checking account** or **savings account**. You might **invest** some by spending money on something that will make you more money in the future. You might worry about having enough for food, clothing, shelter, healthcare, and the well-being of your family. Maybe you'll even give some money away.

You don't have to give your money as much thought at this point in your life as you will when you grow older. Still, knowing how to manage your income, your savings, and your spending money are things you can think about now. One thing you can definitely begin thinking about, and doing, is putting money into a checking or savings account.

Keep on Top of It

Keeping track of your dollars and cents is the best way to make sure you'll always have enough to cover your costs—and enough to have some fun along the way. It all starts with making a plan.

Hey, Big Spender!

What's the first thing you do when you get your allowance, money for doing chores, or a bit of birthday money? Do you run to the mall and blow it on some bling? Do you give it to the local animal shelter? Do you treat all your friends to a movie and munchies?

Those things can be satisfying, but what if you want to buy yourself something big one day? Maybe you've got your eye on a shiny red scooter or a remote-controlled video drone, like the one shown above. How will you ever afford those things if you blow all your dough as soon as it comes in?

The answer is to start managing your money now.

Set Your Goals

Pay Attention!

Did you just yawn at the thought of that? Well, think again. Treat money management like a puzzle that has a variety of pieces that fit together. Or, think about it as a game with lots of levels. Different levels come with different challenges. While some may feel simple enough to pass with your eyes closed, others might be tougher to master.

In the end, though, it's a game you can't lose. You will always be better off when you play the money management game. It means paying attention to your spending, planning your purchases, and setting saving goals. Believe it or not, it can be exciting to figure it all out and watch your money grow!

If you keep your eyes on the prize, you'll be surprised at how quickly you can meet your financial goals—and maybe even buy that fantastic new scooter or video drone sooner than you think.

Never Too Early to Budget

One of the main tools used to organize money is a **budget**. This is a record of where your money comes from (**income**), and where you spend it (**expenses**).

The goal of budgeting is to make sure your income is equal to, or greater than, your expenses. This is called living within your means. Creating and sticking to a

Putting together a budget is a little like assembling a jigsaw puzzle. Each part of your budget is important. Without all the pieces, you won't be able to put together your big financial picture!

budget will also help you reach your financial goals faster than you would without one. Without a budget, you risk running out of money when you need it most.

Before you begin budgeting, you have to gather a bit of information. This is the easy part. All you have to do is track your incoming and outgoing money for a period of time. No changes or decisions required just yet. You just need to observe how money flows into and out of your life.

Follow the Money

You probably already have a good handle on where your money is coming from. Chances are you have only a few sources of spending money right now—your allowance, maybe some birthday bucks, or money you earn for mowing the neighbor's lawn.

Now think about the other side of the equation. Where do you spend your money? This answer may not be quite as clear to you. You might *think* you

FOLLOW THE MONEY

CHIPS

know where your money goes, but if you're like many people, you sometimes spend without even realizing you're doing it. You pay a little bit here, buy a little something there, and before you know it, your wallet is empty.

This spending-without-thinking can lead to financial trouble. That's why it's important to start paying attention to your spending habits now.

Putting The Pieces Together

The beauty of keeping tabs on your income and expenses is that you'll start to see some patterns. You'll discover what sorts of things you usually spend your money on. You'll see how much money you spend in a typical week. You might find that there are things you wish you hadn't spent money on. These are important pieces of the money-management puzzle.

Having a clear picture of how you spend your money now will give you the tools you'll need to figure out how to manage your money as you grow older.

MONTHLY EXPENSES

- FOOD ✓
- ELECTRICITY ☐
- WATER ✓
- PHONE ✓
- INTERNET ☐

IT PAYS TO PAY ATTENTION

Give It a Try, and DIY

Now's a great time in your life to start keeping tabs on your incoming and outgoing money. Tracking your money involves two basic steps—recording where your money comes from and documenting where it goes. A simple financial record has two columns—one for income, one for expenses.

1. Make a chart with two columns: one titled "income," the other titled "expenses."

2. For one week, write down how much money you get and where it comes from in column one. Then, write how much money you spend and where it goes in column 2. At the end of the week, add up each column and compare the two total numbers. Are they equal? Do you have money left over?

3. Make a new chart for the following week. If you have money left over from week one, write that amount in the "income" column for week two. Repeat Step 2 of this activity.

4. Do this for a total of four weeks, with a new chart for each week. Be sure to carry over any money left over from the previous week into the "income" column.

THINK FOR YOURSELF

How Balanced Are You?

You've just completed a set of charts in which you recorded your "income" and "expenses" for every week over a four-week period.

You can see how well you balanced the money you spent with the money you had coming in. Now make some observations:

- Is there a pattern to your income?
- Is there a pattern to your spending?
- Did you underspend or overspend?
- If you overspent on any given week, did it affect how you spent money the following week?
- Did your overall spending habits change because you were paying attention to them? How?

Sock It Away or Pocket It For Play?

After keeping track of your money for a few weeks, it's time to advance to the next level of the financial-planning game: budgeting.

Budgeting begins with asking yourself a few questions about what you want and what you need in life. These are not necessarily the same things. Understanding the difference between the two is important when it comes to making decisions about your dough.

Define Your Wants and Needs

Your wants are the things on your wish list—that awesome red scooter or drone, a comic book or magazine, or a deal on tickets for rides at a nearby amusement park. Wants can be products, activities, or experiences.

Needs, on the other hand, are things you cannot live without—things such as food, clothing, and medication. The rule of thumb is if you can survive or manage without something for a period of time, it's a *want*, not a *need*.

Factor In Your Commitments and Responsibilities

Somewhere in between the wants and needs are responsibilities and **commitments**. For example, making a commitment to join a sports team means you may have to spend money on uniforms or team events—things you don't *need*, but have made a commitment to buy. Or, perhaps you've made an agreement with your parents to contribute to the family cell phone bill every month. That means you have to pay up—or lose your phone. It is your *responsibility* to budget for that money.

Although your financial commitments and responsibilities aren't usually things you need to survive, they should rank in importance closer to your needs than to your wants.

Time To Make Some Decisions

Once you've identified your wants, needs, and financial commitments, it's time to start making choices. Will you blow every buck that comes your way? How will you save up for your mom's birthday gift? How much must you set aside for your cell phone bill? How much spending money will you put in your pocket for fun every week?

These are tough questions. It's important to remember that you, your parents, and other trusted adults are the only ones who should be answering them when it comes to making decisions about your dollars.

What The Experts Might Suggest

It can be helpful to take some tried-and-true advice from financial experts. One thing they suggest is to divide the money you have left over after paying bills into three chunks as soon as it comes in:

1. PAY YOURSELF FIRST.

Set aside 10 percent of all your income in a "rainy day," or emergency, account. The idea is to leave this money untouched and regularly add to it. That way, you have cash on hand for unexpected needs—for example, if you drop your phone into the toilet and need a new one right away.

2. SAVE TO MEET YOUR GOALS.

Into the second pot of money goes the cash you've decided to stash to meet your financial goals—buying that video drone or scooter, for example. Watch this fund grow until you've saved enough to fulfill your goals!

3. HAVE SOME FUN.

After the first two chunks of money are set aside, what's left is your spending money. This is your fun money—what you're able to spend on small daily purchases.

This pie chart illustrates one way you might budget a weekly income of $20. In this plan, you would set aside 10 percent ($2) for your own "rainy day" or emergency fund, and divide the remaining $18 equally between spending money and saving to meet your financial goals.

Weekly income (allowance, chores, babysitting): **$20**

saving to meet your financial goals $9

rainy day $2

spending money $9

Deciding how much money to put in the meeting-your-goals pot versus the fun-money pot can be tricky. It's important to have a balance between your spending and saving. If you save most of your cash, you'll have very little spending money—which can be a quick way to become frustrated and blow your budget. On the other hand, spending too much means your financial goals will take a longer time to reach. Start by making a plan for the money you have, so you can strike that all-important balance.

What Would You Do?

YOUR SMARTPHONE AND YOU

The average cost of a cell phone in 2016 was $261. But the sticker price is not the only cost of using a smartphone. There are so many different deals and arrangements for getting a phone that's it's hard to look at an "average" price for an accurate idea of what it might cost to buy a phone.

One thing we know for sure, though, is that buying the instrument itself is just the start. You will need to pay for accessories, such as a case and earbuds or headphones. Some of the apps you'll want will come at a price. And then, of course, there is the cost of using your phone. These are the numbers that show up on your monthly phone bill, such as the price of your basic service, your data plan, added phones, and government fees.

You can't change the fact that there are charges on your monthly bill that will add to the cost of having a cell phone. There are, however, different companies out there, different plans to choose from, and different options for paying. Here are some of the questions you should be asking when you get to the point of choosing your own plan:

Hi Suzy, here's your bill for this month.

XL	The new Phone Plan X Large 16 GB	$90.00
	Shared data usage	$20.00
📱	Phone 1	$23.99
	Phone 2	$53.91
	Phone 3	$8.16
📄	Surcharges	$11.30
	Taxes and government fees	

$207.36
Due March 2
Autopay March 1

Making sense of all the costs on a monthly cell phone bill is confusing and frustrating, especially if there are several people on the same plan. One thing that's usually *very* clear is that those costs can be a whole lot more than you'd expect!

1. Should I buy an unlimited data plan? Unlimited data usually costs more, but you won't have to worry about paying for exceeding the limits of your plan.
2. Is a prepaid-phone option the way to go? This will limit the use of your phone to an amount you pay ahead of time, helping you avoid higher fees.
3. Do I buy the phone up front, or pay for it using a monthly payment plan? Paying for your phone in monthly installments may be easier because it spreads out the cost of the phone over time. But as with most charges paid over time, you should be sure that there aren't added costs, such as interest, tacked onto every monthly payment.
4. How do I pay my bill—in person, by check or credit card, online, or with an automatic payment from a checking or credit card account? Having your payment made automatically might help you make on-time payments, but you have to make sure you have enough money in your account for the payment.

So... $261 is not the whole story. It may not be your responsibility to pay all these costs at this point in your life. But when the time comes, and you no longer rely on your parents or guardians for financial support, how do you think you'll decide which phone plan works for you—and what you can afford?

Whatever you decide, it will take some digging around online, asking questions of friends and family, and putting your financial smarts to work in making up a budget.

Planning Today, Playing Tomorrow

A smart financial strategy includes setting goals in three different categories:

Short-term financial goals are things you can achieve with the cash you already have. For you, a short-term goal might be to go a to movie with your friends, buy a pair of mittens, or hit a few balls at a batting cage.

Medium-term goals require some saving—perhaps over a few weeks. These goals might include such things as purchasing a funky bike helmet, taking a ski lesson, or buying a chemistry set.

Long-term goals take time to reach. These are expensive items or activities that require you to save for a longer period of time. A tablet, an electric piano, or a pair of designer sunglasses are some examples of long-term goals.

As you grow up your goals will change, and become long term goals. You will eventually need to save for large purchases such as a home, or car, or maybe a college education. Every adult also needs to save for retirement—the time in your life when you stop working.

Although that probably seems far away, it's important to build good financial habits now so that you are able to meet bigger and longer-term financial goals in the future.

Get The Right Kind of Help

If you need help crunching the numbers, ask your parents or guardians for guidance—but probably not your friends, teachers, or, especially, pushy store salespeople!

It will surprise you how quickly your emergency fund and your savings for short- and long-term goals will grow once you have a good financial plan in place. It can be fun to watch your savings grow—and have some left over for spending, too. Most importantly, you'll be setting yourself up for future financial success.

Financing Your Future

Budgeting might sound hard.
Or scary. Or boring.

It can feel overwhelming to start budgeting. Tracking your income, spending, and savings takes time, and sticking to a budget can be challenging! But, over time, budgeting will become a habit. You'll track your dollars instinctively, or without thinking about it. And as you also keep track of what you're saving, you'll happily watch your bank **balance** bloom!

Budgets are meant to change based on your needs, wants, and particular situations. You might come up with a budget, but find that it doesn't work for you once you start following it in your real life. You might not have enough spending money and find yourself saving too much.

Or you may not be reaching your goals as quickly as you want. You can always take a step back and examine your budget to see how it can be adjusted to work for you.

A budget has to fit you, your lifestyle, and your goals. It is meant to be reviewed and changed to find the right balance between spending and saving.

As you grow up, your needs and wants will evolve. Your income and expenses will increase. Your long-term goals will change. Right now, for example, you might want a remote-controlled car. In five to ten years, you'll probably want to buy a real car.

As you get older, the things you budget for will evolve, or change gradually, from what they are now. You'll still be interested in having money for your own entertainment. You will also be considering money for necessities such as rent and other living expenses, transportation, and having money when you retire.

21

Balancing = Juggling

A budget is not something you write down once, then file away forever. Every time your goals, income, or needs change, it's time to juggle the numbers.

There will also be times when you blow your budget. Guaranteed. You might over- or underestimate your income or expenses. You could be faced with an emergency situation that your rainy-day fund doesn't quite cover. Or you might make an **impulse buy** that was a little over your budget.

Don't be hard on yourself when these things happen. Instead, pull out your budget, rearrange a few things, make some choices, and get yourself back on track.

That might mean cutting your snack budget, so you can pay your cell phone bill next month, or skipping that rock-climbing lesson so you can afford a birthday gift for your mom. Because you've been paying attention to where your money comes from and where it goes, you'll know how to juggle things to adjust to your new financial situation.

BE CAREFUL OUT THERE

YOUR PEERS AND THEIR PRESSURE

Sometimes, when you're out shopping with friends, they might try to convince you to buy something you aren't sure about. Say you're browsing boutiques with your buddies, and they urge you to spend way too much money on a designer denim jacket when a regular jean jacket will do. It can be hard to say no when others are jumping on a particular bandwagon.

Sometimes, a pushy salesperson might press you to buy something you don't need. Then there are the "today-only," or "buy-one-get-one-free" sales that put pressure on you to drop some dollars right away. The message is "don't wait—buy now or lose out." Remember, though, there will always be another sale, and another denim jacket.

The final decisions about where and when you spend your dough are up to you. The only people whose opinion you *shouldn't* ignore are your parents or guardians.

You Don't Have To Be Perfect!

Budgeting is not about being perfect. It's about developing good habits, being clear about your financial goals, and making your money work for you.

Learning how to budget is a giant step forward in your financial literacy education. It will help you live within your means and avoid falling into the trap that affects millions of American adults today—the spiral of **debt**.

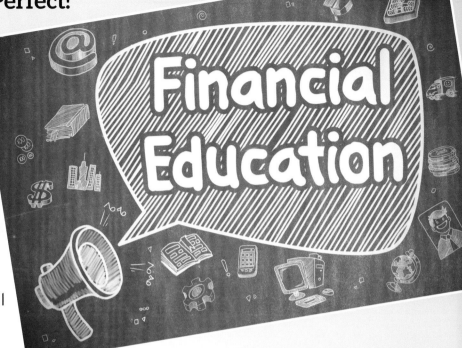

FOCUS ON FINANCE

Saving for the Long, Long, Long Term

Believe it or not, retirement is something that should be on your radar as soon as you start earning a regular income.

In Canada and the United States, people often save for retirement by putting money into retirement savings plans. Many employers also make monthly contributions to retirement plans on behalf of their employees.

Whether you organize a private plan, or take part in a workplace-based retirement program, it's a good idea to contribute to it through automatic payments. That way, your money is set aside before you even see it—you won't even notice it's gone!

Retirement is a long, long way off for you. It might be ten years before you even get your first full-time job. When you get that job, though, you'll know what to do to secure your future. Set up a retirement fund, deposit money every month, and watch it grow!

CHAPTER
THREE

IOU *

More than one-third of American households carry credit card debt. A credit card is a card a person can use to buy things and pay for them at a future date. The ability to make these kinds of purchases leads many people to use credit cards to buy stuff they can't otherwise afford. As of spring 2016, Americans owed a total of $3.6 trillion in credit card bills, student loans, car loans, and other kinds of debt. That's more than $11,000 of debt for every adult and child in the country—and that doesn't even include **mortgages**, the money people borrow to buy homes. The scary part is that one-quarter of Americans are late in their payment of credit card and other bills. Depending on the loan agreement, for every month a bill isn't paid in full, interest may be added, and the consumer falls deeper in debt. This is a stressful cycle and a financially risky way to live. It's also something you *can* avoid.

Using a credit card to make purchases is a convenient way to avoid having to carry around a lot of cash. Not paying off credit card bills in full every month, however, is a sign that you are buying more things than you can afford to pay for. It is also a dangerous way of falling into uncontrollable debt.

* An IOU is a signed document acknowledging a debt that needs to be repaid. "IOU" represents the phrase of "I owe you."

Acceptable Dough To Owe

It's important to note that not all debt is bad. "**Constructive debt**" is money borrowed for a positive reason—to buy a house, to improve your education, to start a business, or to invest in a long-term, moneymaking venture. This is debt that helps improve your financial **status** down the road. It helps you make more money later and actually pay off your debt.

A mortgage is a good example of constructive debt. Taking out a loan to buy a home is a positive step because the home provides the owner with a place to live. In addition, property usually increases in value over time. That means the homeowner will likely sell the home for more money than he or she paid for it in the first place.

Student loans are also considered constructive debt because they help young people improve their education and, therefore, their chances for well-paying jobs down the road.

Being A Borrower In Good Standing

Sometimes people take out loans even if they don't need money. One reason they might do this is to establish a good **credit score**. A credit score is a number that represents a person's likelihood to repay a debt.

Banks and mortgage companies look at a person's credit score to decide whether they will loan that person money. The higher a person's credit score, the more likely it is that he or she will be approved for a loan or a credit card.

If you've never borrowed money or had a credit card, how do you prove you're a good risk for a loan? Some people take out a small loan just to repay it. This helps them establish a good credit score, so future lenders know they're good for the money.

Sometimes, another person (often the parent of a young person) **co-signs** a first loan. That means the co-signer guarantees to pay the money back if the borrower fails to do so.

Investing: Time Is (Usually) On Your Side

Sometimes, people borrow money to invest in long-term opportunities. This is another type of constructive debt.

The goal of investing is to pay money now to earn *more* money later. For example, investors might buy **real estate** (property consisting of land and buildings), knowing it will probably increase in value over time. Or they purchase **stocks**, or shares, in a particular business. Like real estate, these products typically increase in value over time.

The key to investing is to put money into something and leave it there to grow. This usually takes many years. Some people don't want to tie up money they need for their day-to-day expenses, so they borrow money for this purpose.

Keep Your Eyes Wide Open

Borrowing money will mean paying back the original amount of the loan, plus interest. So it is *very* complicated to figure out whether the payoff from long-term investing will be greater than the cost of borrowing money to do so. It's also important to know that every investment comes with the risk that you will lose money instead of raking it in. For these reasons, do *not* borrow money for investing until you have a clear understanding of how it all works.

When Time Is Not On Your Side

Constructive debt is a positive, **proactive** kind of borrowed money. It has its risks, but things such as real estate and stocks usually increase in value over the years. So time is generally a "friend" of this kind of debt. The flip side of that is **destructive** debt. This is the dangerous kind—the kind where time is usually *not* on your side.

Destructive debt is the money people borrow to buy "stuff they think they need"—bling, gadgets, and other cool stuff—but don't have the money to buy.

A consumer often pays a lot of interest, sometimes over a long period of time, to borrow money for these otherwise unaffordable luxuries. This kind of debt can spiral out of control, and even ruin a person's life.

Knowing when—and how much—to invest takes knowledge and patience. Many people with money to invest seek the advice of professional **financial advisers**. These professionals may work for a bank or some other financial organization. Their job is to help you work with financial opportunities in the investment world. They find the best place to put your money. They also weigh such factors as the amount you wish to invest and how long you can wait to let the investment grow.

The Call Of The Credit Card

For many people, destructive debt begins with a credit card. This little plastic rectangle slides easily into a wallet and allows people to buy now, pay later.

Say all your friends are going ice skating, but you've outgrown your skates. You have no cash to buy new ones, but—yay!—you have a credit card in your wallet. You go to the store, choose the perfect skates, and hand over the magic plastic.

It's a super-simple way to buy stuff. It's also a super-simple way to get into debt. With that ice skate **transaction**, you have taken out a loan. The credit card company just paid for your purchase, and you now have a limited period of time to repay it.

If You Wanna Play You've Gotta Pay

It's all good if you pay your credit card bill in full before the due date. If you don't pay up, though, the card company adds interest to the purchase—sometimes as much as 25 percent or more (per year). That means a month after your skate date with your friends, you will owe the credit card company more than the original price of those ice skates.

If that pair of skates is the only thing you ever purchase on a credit card, the debt will be manageable. You might pay it off in a month or two.

Unfortunately, many people say "charge it" too often. They forget, or ignore the fact, that the credit card company is in the business of making money by lending money—not giving gifts to consumers.

Beware the **lure** of the credit card. It doesn't take up much space in your wallet, but it can have a powerful effect, tempting you to buy things you cannot afford.

Don't Try This At Home

Some people get into trouble because they simply don't understand how credit cards work. They get caught up in the buy-now-pay-later concept—and forget the pay-later part. Or, they think the magic plastic card replaces real money.

They might even believe they can buy whatever they want, make the minimum monthly payments, and live the good life! This approach might work for a few months, but credit card companies will eventually come calling for all their cash.

Monthly credit card bills come with a minimum payment option. This is the lowest amount a person has to pay to remain in good standing with the card company. It's usually a small percentage of the balance on the bill. Some people incorrectly believe that the price of their purchase is all they have to pay every month. They forget about that not-so-little thing called interest—a fee that's charged on all of the money they don't pay back every month.

Short-Term Pain, Long-Term Gain

One of the reasons people buy things they can't afford is that they haven't given much thought to their money. They have no short-, medium-, and long-term goals. They have no financial plan. They are thinking in the moment, rather than looking at the big picture.

Sometimes, people see something they want, so they "charge it" without asking if they can afford it. Some people make impulse decisions based on advertising, what their peers are buying, or what they feel they *deserve* to have in life. They give in to the feeling of "I want what I want and I want it now!"

This is called **instant gratification**, and it's the opposite of meeting long-term goals. It's about choosing immediate pleasure, excitement, or fun, at the expense of satisfaction and financial stability down the road.

In the moment, for example, it can be exciting to buy a brand new home theater system. It's not so exciting, though, when the credit card bill arrives a few weeks later, and you can't pay it.

Having a financial plan encourages you to stop, think, and ask yourself a few questions before handing over your credit card. Does this home theater system fit into your big-picture plans? What impact will it have on other choices you've made? If you don't buy it, you might feel disappointed today, but you'll feel great when you take off on that European vacation you've been saving for!

The choice is yours.

A Matter of Interest

Different loans often have different ways of charging interest. Interest is the amount a customer pays for the privilege of using someone else's money, called a loan. The amount of interest charged is usually based on a percentage, or part, of the original loan amount. This is called the **interest rate**. The customer pays interest over the amount of time it takes to pay off the entire loan. The two most common types of interest are simple interest and compound interest.

SIMPLE INTEREST

The most basic type of interest is called simple interest. It is the interest you usually pay when you borrow money for a car or a house.

The pie chart (right) illustrates a used-car loan based on simple interest. In this case, you have borrowed $2,000 at an interest rate of 10 percent. You have agreed with your lender to repay your loan in one year.

Ten percent of $2,000 is $200. In a simple interest loan, that amount is simply added to the original amount you borrowed, called the **principal**. The combined total of principal and interest is $2,200.

As the chart on the right shows, you will repay this amount in a series of 12 monthly payments of a little more than $180 each. At the end of the 12 months, the entire loan, plus interest, will be paid in full.

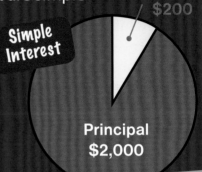

Interest $200

Simple Interest

Principal $2,000

TOTAL AMOUNT PAID OFF OVER 1 YEAR : $2,200

Loan Repaid with Simple Interest
Amount: **$2,000**
Term: **1 year**
Interest rate: **10%**
Total monthly payments: **12**

Principal	Interest	Month	Payment	Balance
$2,000	$200			
				$2,200
		1	$183	$2,017
		2	183	$1,834
		3	183	$1,651
		4	183	$1,468
		5	183	$1,285
		6	183	$1,102
		7	183	$919
		8	183	$736
		9	184	$552
		10	184	$368
		11	184	$184
		12	184	$0

COMPOUND INTEREST

The other kind of interest is called compound interest. This is more complicated than simple interest, and it is the kind that most credit card companies use.

The pie chart (right) shows the same $2,000 principal, but here you are using a credit card with an interest rate of 23.1 percent per year. Not only is the interest rate high, but the card company is charging *compound* interest.

In a loan with compound interest, the interest charge is added every month onto the balance of the principal you have not yet paid off. So the next month, you are charged interest not only on the amount of the principal you still owe but also on the interest from the previous month. That's right—you are charged interest on the interest! Interest that is accumulated quickly until the loan is paid.

You have the option to pay the entire bill in any month, but many people who take out a loan this way make the minimum payments.

This sounds like a nice deal, but there is a catch: Paying the minimum each month will make for a very long, slow, and expensive repayment of your loan.

By making payments of $45 a month, you will take eight and a half years to pay off your loan. You will wind up paying not only the $2,000 principal, but also $2,567 in interest. This means that, by the time you pay off the entire loan, it will have grown to $4,567. That's more than twice the amount of the original principal!

The chart below shows the "progress" of your repayment over eight and a half years, including the interest you pay each year.

Note: The compounded interest you are charged makes it difficult to reduce the monthly balance on your bill. As this chart shows, compounded interest has added $453 to your bill by the end of the first year. If you subtract that $453 from the $540 you paid in monthly payments, you'll see that you have reduced your principal, or beginning balance, for that year by only $87. This leaves you with a large balance of $1,913 at the end of the year.

Compound Interest

Principal $2,000 — Interest $2,567

TOTAL AMOUNT PAID OFF OVER 8.5 YEARS : $4,567

Loan Repaid with Compound Interest
Amount: **$2,000**
Term: **8.5 years**
Interest rate: **23.1% per year (compounded monthly)**
Total monthly payments: **102**

Principal	Year	Interest Paid Yearly	Total Monthly Payments	End-of-Year Balance
$2,000	1	$453	$540	$1,913
	2	431	540	1,804
	3	403	540	1,667
	4	368	540	1,495
	5	323	540	1,278
	6	267	540	1,005
	7	197	540	662
	8	109	540	231
	9	15	247	0

Scary Numbers

By paying the bare minimum, a cardholder still owes the bulk of the borrowed bucks. The next bill—and the next and the next and the next—will include interest on the principal, along with interest on the interest.

Say you buy something for $1,000 on a credit card with an interest rate of 20 percent. If the minimum monthly payment for this amount is $30—and if that's all you pay—it will take *more than eight years* to pay down that bill. During that time, you will pay about $900 in interest, almost doubling the original purchase price.

A Bleak Future Scenario

Now, imagine if you continue to spend, racking up a credit card bill of $10,000, $20,000, or more. You may *never* be able to pay off the credit card.

Some people think this scenario is okay—who cares if they never pay off their purchases when they already have all of the cool stuff they wanted?

Well, credit card companies care. Remember, they are in the business of making money, not handing out freebies. The interest will continue to add up, and the minimum monthly payments will continue to rise.

It's not hard to imagine a terrible scenario in which sooner or later you, the cardholder, won't even be able to make the minimum monthly payment. The card company will come calling to demand its money back—*all* the money. Right now.

Spiraling Out of Orbit

By that time, you will no longer be able to borrow money. Having not paid the credit card debt for months or years, your credit score has tanked. Nobody wants to loan money to someone who doesn't pay it back.

People in this position can lose everything because, at some point, they *have* to pay the money back. This can result in serious consequences. Sometimes, people have to sell possessions to pay back debts. In serious cases, governments might issue an order that a person's paychecks or property is **garnished**, or seized and paid directly toward their debts.

Sadly, this scenario happens every day. Here are some things you should do to avoid it:

- Live within your means.
- Follow a budget that allows you to pay your bills and save a certain amount every month.
- Understand how loans (and interest) work.

In other words, pay attention to your financial literacy lessons! And always remember that credit card companies—and other lenders such as some banks—are only trying to make money.

F CUS ON FINANCE

The Upside of Credit

In some people's hands, credit cards can be trouble. They can lead to serious debt. That doesn't mean they're all bad, though. Used with caution and understanding, a credit card can be a useful tool.

They are good for online shopping—as long as you pay the bill when it comes in. They're also a great way to pay when you have enough money saved to purchase something off your list of long-term goals. Instead of carrying several hundred dollars in cash, you can charge a big purchase to a credit card. The savings are in the bank, so you know you can cover the bill when it arrives. Credit cards are generally accepted as a secondary piece of identification. They can also help an individual—who pays bills on time—develop a good credit score.

Now What?

If you're armed with a solid financial plan, a workable budget, and a healthy financial literacy education, there's a good chance you'll never land deeply in debt. On occasion, though, unforeseen circumstances throw a wrench into the best-laid plans.

A sudden job loss, injury, or other change in income-earning potential can lead to debt. Unexpected expenses may also crop up.

Sometimes, despite all the planning, budgeting, and knowledge, tough financial times come along. And sometimes, despite our best plans, we wind up borrowing in ways that drag us into some bad debt. What do you do when that happens?

The good news is that, if you have a good financial literacy education, you'll know exactly what to do!

Regroup, Reassess, Reevaluate

If you have debt you need to pay off, you should first go to that emergency fund you've been paying into. It's there to help at times like this.

Then you need to make a new financial plan based on the priority of paying off the debt. You'll review your financial goals and create a new budget. Remember, financial planning and budgeting are not one-time activities. They are meant to be reevaluated, fine-tuned, and adjusted whenever anything changes.

You may have to cut expenses, find a way to earn more money, or give up one of your long-term goals. Getting yourself back on solid financial footing should be your goal.

Keep Control of The Situation

The main thing to do is face the debt head on. Gather information. Make sure you know exactly how much money you owe and to whom. How long do you have to pay off the debt? Will the creditor accept small payments over a long period of time, and possibly at a lower interest rate?

Don't be afraid to ask for help. You can speak with trusted adults, and also professionals who are trained to help. A financial adviser or a **credit counselor** can offer sound advice.

The bottom line is that you may have to make changes—but you still have choices.

Your emergency fund gives you something to work with when unforeseen financial hardship strikes. You can put that fund to use as you assemble a new money-management puzzle.

NOT QUITE OFF THE HOOK

Declaring **bankruptcy** is a last resort when it comes to getting out of debt. This is a legal action that gives a person a fresh financial start in life. Sort of.

In Canada and the United States, there are different types of bankruptcy. Full bankruptcy (called Chapter 7 Bankruptcy in the United States and simply Bankruptcy in Canada) frees a person from paying certain debts. On the other hand, it means that person may have to sell many or most of his or her possessions to pay back as much money as possible before the debt is cleared.

This type of bankruptcy stays on an individual's credit record for up to 10 years. It can also affect a person's ability to find a place to live and to obtain services such as electricity, water, phone, and insurance. This is because most organizations are cautious about doing business with people who can't, or don't, pay their bills.

A second type of bankruptcy involves working with a "**Trustees**" to take charge of the unpaid bills and expenses for the debt in question and come up with a repayment plan for some of it. This is called Chapter 13 Bankruptcy in the United States, and a Consumer Proposal in Canada. Not everyone is eligible for this type of arrangement.

This arrangement shows a person's intent to repay the money he or she borrowed. It may involve paying back only a portion of what is owed, however, and it still looks bad on a credit report. It is not something to do lightly.

CHAPTER FOUR
REALITY CHECKS

As you grow up, and your income increases, you'll also start spending more money. At first you might buy a TV for your bedroom, a laptop, or a fancy pair of earrings. A few years from now, you might decide it's time to buy your first car. Eventually, you'll probably rent a place of your own. One day, you might even buy a house, get married, and have children. Each of these new life stages comes with new financial responsibilities—and risks. How do you protect all the people and possessions in your life?

As you move through the stages of your life, you will become increasingly responsible for protecting people, possessions, and activities—from health care and travel to your car, home, personal property, and finances.

Protect
Yourself,
Your Property,
and Others

INSURANCE SERVICES

TRAVEL
LIFE
RESIDENCE
EDUCATION
THEFT
CAR
CANCER
SAVINGS PLANS
MEDICAL
NATURAL DISASTER
HOSPITAL
ACCIDENT
DISABILITY

The Price of Peace of Mind

Sometimes, we experience unexpected events—such as car accidents, injuries, and theft—that can give us some financial challenges. One thing you can do to **minimize** the financial impact of some of those bad things is to buy **insurance**.

Insurance protects you from losing money if something happens to your car, home, business, or health. You can also buy life insurance, travel insurance, and **disability** insurance.

People who buy insurance typically make monthly payments, called **premiums**, to insurance companies. Those payments are pooled with the premiums paid by hundreds of other people. When something bad happens to an insured person, that person submits a request, called a claim, to his or her insurance company to help cover the financial loss. If the loss is covered by the individual's insurance, the company gives that person some of the money from the pool.

Insurance And More Insurance

How much money the insured person receives depends on the contract between the individual and the insurance company. This contract is known as the insurance *policy*. It will be your decision whether to buy most kinds of insurance. It's also up to you to decide how much coverage you need of each kind. This all affects how much you will pay in premiums—a cost you will have to budget for as an adult.

Here are some types of insurance that you will probably consider as you grow older. They should fit your personal needs and lifestyle.

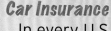

In every U.S. state and the District of Columbia, if you buy a car, you *must* buy some form of car insurance or show proof of being able to pay in case of an accident. Car insurance is **mandatory** in all of Canada.

Car insurance protects you, your car, as well as anyone else involved in the accident and their cars (if the accident is caused by you). Let's say that someone is injured in an accident you have caused with your car. That person might need medical care. Your insurance can cover the cost of that.

Imagine that, as the owner and driver of your car, you get into an accident. (It happens!) Depending on your car insurance policy and the age and value of your car, the insurance company would give you money to help you repair it or buy a new one.

Homeowner's, Renter's, and Business Insurance

Homeowners' insurance will help with the costs of replacing your home and possessions in the case of fire, theft, flood, and many other circumstances. Even if you don't own your own home, you might want to buy renters', or **tenants'**, insurance to protect your possessions.

If you own a business, you might need insurance to cover business losses or to help anyone who is injured while working at your business.

Life Insurance

Life insurance is something you may need if you have **dependents**, or people who would suffer financial hardship if you were no longer around. It's something most people don't like to think about, but it's important. If, for example, a person with children died, how would the children cope financially? A life insurance policy would pay out a sum of money to help them survive.

Health and Disability Insurance

Health insurance helps with medical expenses. Disability insurance also does that. In addition, disability insurance provides an income if a person is unable to work because of an injury or other health-related reason.

Travel Insurance

Travel insurance is a type of protection people sometimes buy when they go on vacation. It can cover everything from lost luggage to flight cancelations to medical emergencies while a traveler is out of town.

Most health insurance policies cover medical care for illness and accidents. These policies also usually provide payment for follow-up visits to your physician, physical therapist, and other providers of medical care.

BE CAREFUL OUT THERE

WHO YOU GONNA CALL?

When you need financial advice in life, trust the experts and those who know your situation best. Your friend might have a "get-rich-quick" suggestion for you, or your cousin's cousin might know of a "can't-lose" investment opportunity. These people might mean well, but it's best not to depend on your buddies to tell you what to do with your money. What is right for them might not be right for you.

Today, your parents and guardians are the only people you should turn to for help with money decisions. As you grow up, it's a good idea to find a respected financial adviser who has your best interests at heart. Remember, though, the final decisions about your money are up to you. You are the one responsible for your financial situation.

There If You Need It

In short, insurance is a sort of safety net. You may never need it, but if you have it, you will be protected financially if things go wrong.

Some types of insurance are required, such as car insurance. Others are a choice. But having certain kinds of insurance—just in case—is a good idea. It can give you peace of mind, knowing you'll have help when you need it.

When the time comes for you to consider insurance—say, for your possessions when you move out of your parents' home—you should remember to research the policies you're considering. For example, you may already be covered for certain things under your parents' insurance. Or perhaps an insurance plan has too much or too little coverage for your needs. Be sure to think carefully before you commit yourself to a policy.

LESSONS LEARNED

In this book, you've learned about the importance of having a financial plan and budget that are updated whenever your financial circumstances change. You've also learned about debt—how to stay out of it, and what to do if you get into it.

These are the things *you* can do to make sure you're financially sound for life—but there are outside factors that can also influence your bank account.

Have you ever heard your parents say something like this: "I can't believe that candy bar costs one dollar. When I was your age, it was only twenty-five cents."

Prices increase over time. This is an example of **inflation**. Inflation is a constant in life—the value of goods and services is guaranteed to increase over the years. Just how much prices will rise is the unknown factor. A person's income typically grows over time, too, but it might not grow as quickly as the cost of goods and services.

This is where planning your financial future can get tricky. Say you plan to have one million dollars in the bank by the time you retire from your career. By today's standards, that's a good financial situation. By the time you're ready to retire, though—50 years from now—one million dollars won't go as far. By then, you might need 1.5 million dollars or more to live comfortably for the rest of your life.

The **economy** of your country, state, province, or town can also influence your financial position. The economy is related to **supply and demand** of products and services.

Say you live in a town where most people work at a car factory. When the demand for cars is high, there are lots of jobs, and people have lots of money to spend at the town's shops and businesses. The economy is healthy. When the demand for cars drops, though, people might lose their jobs and have little money to spend. This is a weak economy.

Inflation and the economy are things you have no control over—but with financial literacy education, you'll be prepared for changes they may cause. You'll know exactly how to handle any financial twists and turns life throws at you.

Understanding how money works, and how it can work for you, is the (not-so-secret) secret to having choices and financial freedom in life.

Inflation is the increase, over time, in the cost of a wide variety of goods and services, such as food, bicycles, cars, education, and homes.

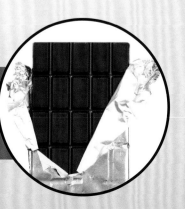

GLOSSARY

app Short for "application"; a program or piece of software, as on a computer, smartphone, or tablet, designed to perform a particular task or service for the user

automatic payment A regular payment that an account holder authorizes the bank to take out of an account to pay another person or business

balance The amount of money due on a bill or a loan; mathematically, the balance is the difference between the amount owed and an amount paid

bankruptcy The legal declaration that a person cannot pay his or her debts

budget (noun) An estimate of how much money comes in and goes out of a household or business in a given period of time; the amount of money needed or available for a purpose, such as running a household

check A written order directing a bank to pay money from a customer's account

checking account An account at a bank from which payment can be made for checks written by the person to whom the account belongs

co-sign To sign a document with another person to agree to share the responsibility for a contract or loan

commitment An obligation; something a person has agreed to do

constructive debt Money borrowed for a positive reason, such as increasing one's wealth or improving one's lifestyle or career; mortgages and student loans are examples of constructive debt

consumer Someone who buys a product or pays for a service

credit card A card with which a person can buy things and pay for them later

credit counselor A person who advises others on money matters relating to debt

credit score A number on a scale that indicates how likely a person is to repay a loan

data plan A monthly subscription to a carrier for smartphones, tablets, or other wireless devices that provides access to email, apps, the internet, and other services that require an online connection

debt Money owed to a person or organization

dependent A person who relies on someone else for financial and other support

destructive Causing harm or damage

disability A condition that limits a person's movements, senses, or activities

economy The system of how money is made and used within a particular country or region; the economy is connected with things such as how many goods and services are produced and how much money people can spend on them

expense The amount of money something costs

financial adviser A person who helps other people manage and invest their money

garnish To seize (usually money or property) to pay off a debt or a claim

impulse buy A purchase made without thinking, spur-of-the-moment

income Money earned or otherwise acquired

inflation A general increase in prices, often accompanied by a decrease in the value of money to make purchases

instant gratification Immediate happiness, pleasure, or satisfaction

in areas such as health, disability, or auto, home, and business ownership; customers pay regular fees to an insurance company, which covers customers' costs when the need arises

interest A fee paid to borrow someone else's money

interest rate A portion of an amount owed, usually expressed as a percentage, that determines how much interest is added to the original amount

invest To purchase something now to make money in the future

loan Something that is borrowed, especially money, that is expected to be paid back, usually with interest

long-term goal Something a person wants to do or buy in the future

lure Something that can be used to tempt someone to do something, often by offering some kind of a reward

mandatory Required by rule or law; compulsory

medium-term goal Something a person wants to do or buy soon but not right away

minimize To reduce to the smallest amount possible

mortgage A loan to buy a home

paycheck-to-paycheck A situation in which a person or family meets all financial obligations with current earnings from one pay cycle to the next, needing all those earnings to survive until the following payday

premium An amount of money paid to buy insurance; insurance premiums are often paid in the form of payments made on a regular basis, such as monthly or yearly

principal The original amount of money that was borrowed

proactive Taking action to control or change a situation, rather than waiting until it happens and reacting to it

real estate Land and buildings permanently attached to a piece of land

retire To leave one's job, usually upon reaching a certain age or time of life when one might stop working

savings account An account at a bank into which money is deposited; the purpose of most savings accounts is to keep money handy but not as needed for daily expenses, and to earn small amounts of interest

short-term financial goal Something a person wants to do or buy very soon

status Social or professional rank

stocks Shares in businesses or companies

supply and demand How much of a good or service is available (supply) and how much people want it (demand); these factors contribute to the price of goods and services

taboo Forbidden; prohibited or restricted by social custom

tangible Capable of being perceived by the senses, especially by touch

tenant A person who occupies or uses land or property owned by someone else

transaction An exchange of goods, services, or money

trustee A person who is responsible for managing someone else's property or money

FURTHER INFORMATION

BOOKS

Butler, Tamsen. *The Complete Guide to Personal Finance: For Teenagers and College Students* (revised second edition). Ocala, FL: Atlantic Publishing Group, Inc., 2010.

Chatzky, Jean. *Not Your Parents' Money Book*. New York: Simon & Shuster Books for Young Readers, 2010.

Dakers, Diane. *The Bottom Line: Money Basics* (Financial Literacy for Life). Crabtree Publishing, 2017.

Dakers, Diane. *Getting Your Money's Worth: Making Smart Financial Choices* (Financial Literacy for Life). Crabtree Publishing, 2017.

Maybury, Richard J. *Whatever Happened to Penny Candy?* Bluestocking Press, 2015.

WEBSITES

www.themint.org/
The Mint is a website designed to teach financial literacy skills to kids, teens, parents, and teachers. It includes information, games, and tools to help you learn. Here are a trio of links about credit cards, debt, and insurance:

www.themint.org/kids/credit-card-facts.html

www.themint.org/teens/owing.html

www.themint.org/teens/safeguarding.html

http://read.marvel.com/#/labelbook/41238
This link takes you to a free graphic novel, *Guardians of the Galaxy: Rocket's Powerful Plan*. In this book, Ant-Man, Hulk, Black Widow, and others join the Guardians in a money-saving adventure.

www.moneyandyouth.cfee.org/en/
This website, called *Money and Youth: A Guide to Financial Literacy*, is for kids and grown-ups who want to learn about finances. It includes a full glossary, links to other sites, and an excellent Q&A section. It also offers a link to a free, and excellent, e-book.

www.pbskids.org/itsmylife/money/index.html
It's My Life: Money is an informative site created by PBS Kids. It is divided into three sections–Making Money, Spending Smarts, and Managing Money. Each topic includes information, discussions, and tools to help you learn about your money.

www.practicalmoneyskills.com/personalfinance/creditdebt/
The Practical Money Skills website, features games, information, and resources for all ages. This particular link takes you to the Credit & Debt section.

INDEX

ABOUT THE AUTHOR

Diane Dakers was born and raised in Toronto, and now makes her home in Victoria, British Columbia. She has written three fiction and 18 nonfiction books for young people. During her career, Diane has worked full time, part time, on contract, and on-call. She is currently self-employed. She has earned money in the form of wages, salaries, royalties, scholarships, and investment income. She loves spreadsheets!